Newton Ferrers and Noss Mayo Remembered

Arthur L. Clamp

PART 2

The Creek is partly Frozen

It is January, 1954, and in the middle of a very cold spell of weather. The children are taking advantage of a new activity. Katherine Crocker, Kerry Bradley, Pat Thomas, Rosalind Prynn and William Prynn are enjoying themselves a few yards from their school.

This version of the book is virtually as originally published.
There are now additional pages at the back providing information about the author.

The republishing project is being managed by Arthur's grandson, Steven Gibson. We aim to find all the research that he was involved in publishing, preserving it for the next generation as part of 'The Clamp Collection'.

THE FISHING TRADE OF NEWTON AND NOSS

It appears that about half of the inhabitants of Newton and Noss were engaged in fishing in one way or another when this means of earning a livelihood was at its height. No doubt fishing has taken place from the Yealm estuary for hundreds of years but it was during the latter half of the last century that about half of the community were dependent on regular fishing, a time when Lord Revelstoke had the baulking stores built in which the catches could be salted and stored for later sale.

Mr. Edgar Foster tells me that there were twenty-seven double-handed crabbers with a few single-handed boats, and six drifters working out from here at the turn of the century. The drifters had ceased by about 1912 but it was the social upheaval of the First World War that brought about the decline of the trade as many local men did not return from the trenches or they moved away in search of alternative work. Crabbers worked during the 1920s and 1930s slowly falling in number and with the outbreak of the 1939-45 war this finally closed the life-long activity of the estuary. He said that a Mr. Bob Andrews and Mr. Jack Shepherd, working for awhile in the late 1950s, were the last bonafide local fishermen. Other men did continue however, but not as a full-time occupation as the local waters could be easily worked by the growing number of large boats based in the Barbican, Plymouth. There is still fishing taking place mainly for sport and perhaps earning a little from time to time when the weather and sea is good.

The crabbing season always started on Valentine's day, 14th February, unless it fell on a Sunday and then it took place as near to this day as possible. Men went out six days a week but never on a Sunday. This was set aside for attendance at the local chapel and churches a practice kept up until the 1930s.

Crabs and lobsters were mainly caught on the East and West Rutts, a series of underwater rocks, which had to be worked during slack water, a period of about two hours when pots could be easily raised, rebaited and lowered. The tide almost always determined the working day as it took about five to six hours to complete the full trip out to the grounds men rowing their boat or using the usual sprit and foresail when there was sufficient wind. It was customary to get out of the harbour by first light, returning around mid-day, storing the catch in pots kept close to Wide Slip where the crabbers were moored in line and then spending the rest of the day maintaining equipment and working on boats.

There were about thirty pots to be hauled up when an average of fifteen to twenty crabs and lobsters would be deftly taken out of them, some having two or three in, and quickly checked to see that they were not below the required 9 inches for lobsters and 5 inches for crabs in size. There was larger shell fish about but they could not enter the 9 inch hole at the top of the pots.

The fishermen made their own pots producing about three times the required number as many would get lost, damaged or clawed through by the shell fish. They were made from willows grown on any marshy ground by local farmers. The stored crabs and lobsters would be raised and taken into the Barbican for the 7 a.m. fish market although some would also be sold locally.

The crabbing boats averaged between 18 to 23 ft. in length, were built locally by a Mr. John Hockaday costing in the region of £12, while some came from Chances of Salcombe who built boats for many fishermen of the south west. They were rigged in such a manner that the sails could be quickly and easily stored during raising and shooting of the pots.

Of the six drifters which Edgar Foster can recall, the *Mayflower* belonged to Mr. Hockaday, the *Forrester* to Mr. Leonard, the *Sophia* and *Glance* to the licensee of the *Dolphin Inn,* William Roach, who allowed the boats to be hired out. They were crewed by three or four men drift-netting mainly for pilchards much further out and along to Bigbury Bay. Each had a main sail and mizzen sail and were in use from about September to February after which they were moored on the estuary mudflats for the rest of the year.

The catch was normally taken to the baulking stores where the pilchards were pressed between layers of salt in small barrels for storage and eventual sale at Plymouth although he can recall some being exported as far away as Italy. Local families often brought fish from the store and cured it themselves in readiness for the winter months. The stores also held equipment and after its closure as a fish-curing building, was converted into living accommodation and general stores.

For a short time the drifters also took out vegetables and mail to the keepers in the Eddystone lighthouse and the *Dolphin Inn* was the official mail box for correspondence for them.

ACKNOWLEDGEMENTS

I am greatly indebted to many people for responding to my suggestion in the first illustrated booklet for more photographs of this locality. The response soon resulted in this collection making more pages than the first title! My thanks must be expressed to Mr. E. Foster, Mrs. A. Redfern and Mr. G. Hockaday for their substantial help and encouragement towards this end.

Arthur L. Clamp,
203 Elburton Road,
Plymouth, Devon.

Calm waters of the Estuary

What looks like young visitors to Newton have probably hired this rowing boat for an hour or so carefully taking it up towards a landing point at Newton. The date is sometime around 1930 and the village has yet to see the great many changes that came within a decade or so of this photograph being taken from an accompanying boat.

Hookers of Yealm Estuary

Edgar Foster has identified two of the three hookers which worked from the Yealm, these craft being able to get further out to sea than the smaller crabbers where longlining and hook and line fishing took place. The hooker on the left is the *Ida* owned by George Foster and built at Looe in 1900 by a Mr. Ferris. Another is on the far right, *Little Aggie*, and the third was called *RSE* owned by H. Hockaday. The centre vessel is a yawl-rigged yacht.

A Walk to Passage Woods

Then the only likely means of getting around was on foot. The two ladies and child appear to be starting out on an afternoon's stroll. The low building on the right was then used by William Hockaday, the Tilley Institute (established 1843) had its rounds of billiards, snooker and used as a meeting place and in the cottages ahead lived Mr. Hockaday, Harold Sims, a fisherman, and Mr. Penwell. The period is around the 1914 era.

Crabbers below Riverside Road West

Mr. Sitters then lived in *Elmtree Cottage*, Mr. and Mrs. Hereford in *Vine Cottage*, the Collings family in *Jasmine* and Mr. and Mrs. H. Phillips in *Virginia Cottage*. Above them stands *Mewstone, Elstow, Cam Cottage, Haws Park* and the fields of Court Farm then run by Mr. R. Kingcombe.

Off Fishing
The bait box on the side of the small boat gives the clue to what is about to happen. Harry Foster often went out with his father in *Snowdrop* crabbing but here he is close to the Point at high water and ready for a day's fishing.

Harry Foster at Work
This very faded photograph of about 1912 shows him working on an oar outside his workshop and store at No. 54 Noss Mayo. A variety of tackle and ropes, etc. hang from the walls of the old building.

Local People and a Visitor
George and Bessie Foster pose in their garden for this photograph dated around 1914. He was a fisherman owning the *Snowdrop* and played the organ in Noss chapel. The unknown visitor is clearly recognised by his white clothes resting against a boat at the quay below Ferry Cottage.

Outside No. 54 Noss Mayo

Fisherman George Foster poses for the camera outside this building which he later bought. One of the well known people of the area he gained his living by crabbing; one of his willow pots is lying by his side. The date of this photograph is not known.

Ivy-clad Post Office

This very early view of the old building was taken from the creek with St. Peter's tower behind. Called *Foster's Ye Olde Original Stores*, many will remember this shop which served the immediate locality. Note what looks like sacks drying on the boat.

Four Boys and a Toy Boat

They have not been identified but they are enjoying themselves at half tide close to the *Foss* at Noss creek. The year is sometime in the 1940s.

Ancient Order of Foresters

Harry and his son Sydney proudly wear their membership sashes of this friendly society which met once a month in the Tilley Institute.

A New Noss Mayo Post Office

This was built in 1926 in front of the old building and remained in use until about 1948 as a post office and 1967 as a shop. Hettie and Harry Foster ran it assisted from time to time by local people two of whom are seen below with their aprons on with two other people.

Grandma Hodge

A very familiar figure at Noss, she spent her eighty years in the village and was the wife of George skipper of the *Kitley Belle*. She died in 1932.

West View, Newton Hill

The home of the West family for about a 100 years and seen here are Edward, Ernest, Sidney, Charles, Bert and Ethel and the year is about 1914. Jack West was the last of the family to live here up until the 1970s.

Stores and Post Office
The drinking tap can be seen used by the nearby householders and also by people visiting the area by boat. The stores became the post office well before 1914 and remained so until the building was demolished in the middle 1920s.

Ye Olde Original Stores
This is the earliest view of the thatched building long used as the village stores for Noss Mayo. William Roberts was here in the 1880s but George Foster is better known for running it from at least 1897 to 1926 if not later.

A Motorcycle made for Two!
Cecil Daymond has allowed Sydney Foster and his aunt Hetty Foster to sit on his James motorcycle outside the old post office at Noss. He was the organist at the church for some years.

The Shop Closes
Lilian Foster stands in the front of her shop which closed 30th September, 1967. It then became a yacht chandlers for awhile but this business ceased in 1981 and the front part of the building converted to a private house now occupied by Mr. and Mrs. W. Redfern.

George Foster's Shop

He is recorded being here as early as the mid-1890s some years before this photograph was taken. The old building with its thatched roof stood at the bottom of Pillory Hill. A horse and trap is at the top while two boys watch curiously as Mr. Foster, with two grandchildren, pose by the entrance to the shop.

Lots 53 and 54

Much valuable information can be obtained from these entries in the 1915 sale catalogue of the Membland Estate. The *Swan Inn* and Mr. George Foster's shop, as shown above, were both purchased by their tenants.

Lot 53. (Coloured Pink on Plan No. 2.)

The "Swan Inn"

Is entirely "free" has a full seven day's License, and is No. 73 on plan.

It comprises:—Bar Parlour, Kitchen, Tap Room and Bar, Cellar, Bed Room with Sitting Room adjoining and Two other Bed Rooms.

Good Garden and a Large Stone and Slated Store Shed along side the Creek.

Let to Mr. N. G. Bunker on a yearly tenancy at a rental of **£20** per annum.

Outgoings: Tithe Commutation Rent Charge, Vicarial 1 11
Tenant pays rates. Impropriate 1 2
3 1 Value 1915 2s. 4½d.

Lot 54. (Coloured Blue on Plan No. 2.)

General Shop and House

built of Stone, with Thatched Roof, and being No. 55 on Plan.

It contains Large Shop, Sitting Room and One Bed Room, lean-to Larder. Also a large Store Room, with small Garden situated adjoining the Noss Creek.

Let to Mr. G. Foster on a yearly tenancy at a rental of £10 per annum.

A portion of the Store Room is used as an Estate Workshop and the underneath portion is let to Mr. G. Hodge, Senr. with other Lands on a yearly tenancy at an apportioned rental of £1 5s. per annum, producing in all **£11 5s.** per annum.

Outgoings: Landlord pays rates.

The Swan Inn and Stores

Nicholas Bunker was the innkeeper here as recorded in 1910 and 1926 local directories. The brick-arched tap was the water supply and the wall on the left is where the small car park is. Who was the young girl on the scooter just at the corner of the inn?

Noss School Children in the 1920s

They pose for the photographer outside the Tilley Institute with their teacher and Sidney Foster, Doris Northcott, Cyril Mashford and Fred Mashford, have been identified. Others will be likely to be recognised some of whom are still living in this area.

Yealm United A.F.C. 1919-20

The first team are posed for the camera made up of Arch Tope, Gordon Bunker, Ned Richards, Alf Roach, Sid Andrews, Ralph Kingcombe, Ernest Rogers, Joe Hisbent, Phil Hockaday, Fred Algar, Vince Hodge, Cecil Lake, Bill Hazeller, George Mears, Bill West, Jack Hodge and Norman Wyatt.

An Earlier Group of Children

The style of dress suggests that this picture dates around 1910 and again shows one of the teachers of Noss School surrounded by her class of twenty-four children. Of interest are the heavy boots the boys are wearing and the girls with their white pinafore dresses.

A Mixed Band

Sashes and white dresses enhance this group of local players who often entertained the villagers during the 1920s. Cecil and Allen Daymond have been recognised but regrettably no others. However, the musical talent of these people will be remembered and jog memories of these delightful occasions.

In front of the Village Hall

Most children like dressing up and these from Noss Mayo primary school are no exception. Here Andrew Trout, Joyce Gosling, Susan Roberts, Trevor Finch, Sylvia Delafield, Rosemary Codd, Ann Foster and Paul Pearson proudly display themselves in the various costumes.

Noss Mayo Primary School

The children are taking part in the nativity tableau in St. Peter's Church, 1952. They are Trevor Finch, Joyce Gosling, Sylvia Delafield, Ann Foster, Sian Thomas, Betty Pearse, Paul Pearson, Rosemary Codd, Andrew Trout, Peggy Treneman and Janet Gosling.

Looking towards Bridgend

A young girl is walking along the road here sometime before 1914 when Mr. and Mrs. Reed lived in one of the thatched cottages and a Miss Gill. Mr. John Rowe and Mr. Lugger worked at one time in the malthouse where barley was brought in from local farms and made into malt in preparation for brewing in Plymouth. The corn was laid out to dry on the floors of the house and wooden shovels used to turn it over.

The Greybacks at Rest

This pre-1900 photograph shows St. Peter's Church (opened in 1882) with fields around it, four greyback boats on the mudbanks below and Point House on the other side of the water. The roof of the building in the foreground is at the end of Riverside Road West.

At the Head of the Creek

This early view of Noss clearly shows the Tilley Institute and the old village school. This was opened in 1839 for 200 children and at the time of this photograph James Harrison was the headmaster. There was then an average attendance of 105 pupils. The Tilley Institute dates from 1843 with an extension in 1878 and at this time, 1914, William Payne was given as the librarian. It is recorded that about 600 books were presented to the institute or reading room by Lord Revelstoke some years previously.

A Broader view of Noss Mayo

This photograph was probably taken at the same time as the above showing almost the whole of the village with houses and the chapel in the foreground. The Wesleyan chapel dates from 1870 and is inscribed with the letters TL on its foundation stone. Harry Bidgood was then at the *Globe Inn*, some of the fields then belonged to Coombe Farm run by Robert Baskerville and James Penwell, one of two local carriers to Plymouth, lived in one of the cottages to the left of the inn.

Sunday School Group
This group photographed about 1904 shows Miss Hettie Foster, teacher, with the very smartly dressed youngsters assembled from the chapel probably on the occasion of an anniversary.

A family Group
Here the fisherman George Foster with his half waders on sits with his grandson George, his wife Elizabeth, son Henry George, daughter in law Jenny, standing, and daughter Henrietta (Hetty) sitting.

A Year Later
A closer view is obtained in the lower group recorded about a year later with Hettie Foster, again in the middle, wearing a straw boater hat. Bertram, Ada and Olive Revel, George Foster and Beattie Horton have been recognised. Note the crab pot on the left.

The Finest Paddle Steamer
The *Alexandra* is here on the Yealm about 1925 with passengers out from Plymouth for the day. This vessel was then owned by the Plymouth Piers, Pavillion and Saltash Three Towns Steamship Co., Ltd. and is moored in the Pool off Wide Slip. She was built in 1888 and was the largest purpose-built local passenger boat sailing on waters around Plymouth.

The beloved Kitley Belle
This well-remembered small vessel carried passengers up and down from Steer Point. She is here moored off Wide Slip and curiously has all her four cabin windows open, not a normal practice.

Landing Passengers
George Hodge is skilfully landing passengers from the *Kitley Belle* at Steer Point sometime in the early 1920s. Hundreds of people must have used this means of transport in getting to and from Newton and Noss during the first three decades of this century.

Steer Point Slip
Someone was thoughtful enough to record this once very common sight of local people on their way to Plymouth first by the favourite *Kitley Belle* then by train from the nearby Steer Point station. An alternative landing was just around the corner and both are still there with their slipways.

Wesleyan Chapel Annual Outing

Annual outings have always been well supported and this large group of people out from Noss Mayo, probably in the late 1920s, is typical of young and old enjoying themselves for the day. The beach is either at Old Cellars or Mothercombe to which they walked or went by horse and cart. Harry Foster and George Foster, the organist at the chapel, have been identified.

Yealm United Second Team in the early 1920s

Recognised here are George Hockaday, Sam Shepherd, Cecil Lake, Harold Sims, Olf Shepherd, Les Roach, Bill Crook, Stewart Squires, Bill Hockaday, Jack Tope, Vince Hodge, Joe Hisbent (who played for Arsenal and Aston Villa) and Bob Baker among others not identified.

158 PH Snowdrop

Three generations of the Fosters: Young Georgie sitting on the bow of the crabber *Snowdrop* with her father, Henry George (Harry) and grandfather George at Noss Creek. The boat was built at Salcombe and owned by George. Note the other boats in the backtground of this picture taken sometime before the First World War.

At Pope's Quay in 1925

George Foster about to go out in his small rowing boat probably to his much larger boat the crabber *Snowdrop*. The crabs caught would be sold in the Barbican, Plymouth.

A Maun of Bait

The old fishermen are standing close to Noss Voss with a basket or "maun" showing part of a ray hanging over its edge. This was used for bait and may well indicate that they are about to go out fishing. Harry Foster, Sydney, his son, and George Foster, who used to preach at the chapel, make up the group behind which is a crabber.

George Reeve

He was the caretaker of the Tilley Institute for some years and is here putting a weight on his mooring line for the boat.

William Leonard

Edgar Foster has identified him rowing across high water at Noss creek towards the *Swan Inn* and the landing point below the Hodge's family house.

Taylor's Quay

Known by this name by the local fishermen years ago, boats are still launched here at the end of Riverside Road West. This pre-1914 picture shows three crabbers, the one on the right with a "bunkin" at its bow to take a larger area of sail. Mr. H. Phillips ran a twice weekly market boat from here to Plymouth roundabout this period.

High Tide below Ferry Cottage

Passengers are about to be taken over on the ferry a service which has been working for many years from this spot. George Hockaday was the ferryman for a while, assisted by his daughters, then there was Len Carter.

Lot 13. (Coloured Pink on Plan No. 1.)

" Ferry Cottage "

Is built of Stone and Brick with Slated Roof and situated on the bank of the River Yealm, and having beautiful views.

It contains Two Bed Rooms, Kitchen and Wash-house. There is a Small Verandah with a Tea Room underneath.

Adjoining is a Three-stall Stable with a Bedroom over.

Let to Mr. R. Mashford on a yearly tenancy at a nominal rental of

per £5 annum.

Included in this Lot are Two Small Willow Plots, let to Messrs. J. H. Sims and W. Leonard, Jun., at yearly rentals of 7s. 6d. and 2s. 6d. respectively

Outgoings :
Tithe Commutation Rent Charge, Vicarial 1s. Value 1915 9d.

Sale of Ferry Cottage

The sale of the very large Membland estate in Plymouth in 1915 enabled many local people to buy the properties they were living in. Lot 13, Ferry Cottage, was one of many dwellings sold in Noss and it is interesting to see how much it made as pencilled by Mr. Wakeham, the farmer at Rowden, who was at the sale.

Low Tide below Ferry Cottage

This shows the jetty and small quayside below the cottage, the place for crossing the estuary, and where an occasional yacht would be cleaned in the manner of the one shown here. The inverted barrel with the word "private" on it suggests that anyone could not land here. The old baulking stores, built at the expense of Lord Revelstoke, are on the far bank.

1862

REVELSTOKE, with the village of Noss Mayo, is a parish nine miles S.E. of Plymouth, containing 1,478 acres of land. Crabs, lobsters, herrings, and other kinds of fish are caught here in abundance. The church, an ancient edifice, is in a very dilapidated state. The living is a perpetual curacy, annexed to the vicarage of Yealmpton. There is a Chapel of Ease at Noss Mayo, erected in 1840. There is a small National school, erected by subscription and a grant from Government, supported by subscription and the payments of the children.

TRADERS, &c

Anthony, James, farmer
Anthony, Richard, farmer
Bunker, Richard, shoemaker
Carter, Joseph, blacksmith
Huxham, George, farmer
Kingcombe, Henry, oyster merchant
Popham, Humphrey, shopkeeper
Tuckett, James, farmer
Willcocks, John, farmer

NOSS MAYO.

Giles, Mr. S., master, R.N.
Walker, Mr. Andrew

TRADERS, &c.

Cann, William, National schoolmaster
Crocker, Henry, carpenter
Elliott, Sarah, beer retailer
Kingcombe, John, farmer
Leonard, John, tailor
Perrett, Philippa, shopkeeper
Pope, William, carpenter
Roe, John, Globe Inn
Reeves, Frederick, shoemaker
Sherrell, William, Swan
Williams, John, shopkeeper

Lists of Local People

A great source of local information can be obtained from the many trade directories produced during the past 100 years. They give a valuable insight into the businesses and trades of the year. Those shown here are for 1850, 1865, 1870 and 1897.

1870

NEWTON FERRERS is a village and parish in Plympton St. Mary union, containing, by the census of 1861, 670 inhabitants, and 3191 acres; in the deanery of Plympton, archdeaconry of Totnes, diocese of Exeter, hundred of Ermington, South Devonshire, on the banks of the river Yealm, about 2 miles from the sea coast, and 7½ south-east from Plymouth. The rectory, in the patronage and incumbency of the Rev. John Yonge, M.A., had the tithes commuted, in 1839, at £440 per annum, with residence and 88A. 3R. 6r. of glebe land. The church is an ancient edifice in the later English style, dedicated to the Holy Trinity, consisting of nave, chancel, north and south aisles, and tower with five bells. There are National Schools for children of both sexes. There are some small charitable bequests for the benefit of the poor, and some almshouses which are not endowed. John Holberton, Esq., is lord of the manor.

Clergy and Gentry.

Chaffe Mr. H.
Depore Miss
Harris Mr. W.
Middleton William, Esq., Torr house
Penphrase Alexander, Esq.
Sholl Miss
Stewart Admiral Sir Austin, Gnaten hall
Tonkin Henry, Esq., Buffords Newton
Yonge Rev. Duke, M.A., curate, Court house
Yonge Rev. John, M.A., rector, Puslinch

Trades and Professions.

Baker Wm., blacksmith, Bridge end
Barratt Richard, farmer, Torr
Brown William, shoemaker, Bridge end
Button Francis, farmer, Westcombe
Chaffe Richard, farmer, Court
Cornthwaite Charles, farmer, Collaton
Dawe Henry, farmer, Clannacombe
Edmunds Robert, basket maker
Edwards Wm., farmer, Newton downs
Fowler John, shoemaker
Hodge H., shoemaker and shopkeeper
Jones William, carrier, Torr
Knight Thomas, tailor
Knight Thomas, jun., mason
Leonard Philip Quick, parish clerk and sub-postmaster
Loye John, shoemaker
Luscombe Robert, farmer, Preston
Matthews Richard, farmer, Creber
Matthews William, farmer
May Jonathan, farmer, Broadmoore
Parsons Thomas, thatcher
Rowe John Martin, "Dolphin" inn
Rowe Richard, carpenter
Saunders Philip, farmer, Ashcombe
Steer Edmund, farmer
Stephenson William, carpenter
Thorning John, pilot
Tope William, carpenter
Wilcock Joseph, farmer, Lolesbury
Wills Richard, farmer, Torr
Winter John, farmer, Bridge end

Post Office.—Philip Q. Leonard, sub-postmaster. Letters from Ivybridge arrive at 9.55 a.m.; dispatched at 2.40 p.m. Yealmpton is the nearest money order office

National School.—Mrs. Elizabeth Honey, mistress

REVELSTOKE parish has its church on the sea coast, near Stoke Point and Bigbury Bay, but most of its inhabitants are in the large fishing village of NOSS MAYO, which lies in a low situation, on the south side of a creek from the mouth of the Yealm, opposite Newton Ferrers, nine miles S.E. of Plymouth. Crabs, lobsters, herrings, and other fish are caught at Noss Mayo, where the villagers suffered severely from *cholera* in 1849, when about 50 of them died, and more than 200 were afflicted with the dreadful malady. Liberal subscriptions were made for the relief of the sufferers, and a medical gentleman was sent down from London to their assistance. The parish had 613 inhabitants in 1841, and contains 1470A. 2R. 19P. of land. The manor of Revelstoke was long the property and seat of the Revells, and was sold about 12 years ago, by Sir J. Perring, to its present owner, Robert Robertson, Esq., of Membland. W. W. Pendarves, Esq., owns the manor of Lambside, and part of the parish belongs to a few smaller owners. The *Church* is an ancient structure, with a small belfry and two bells; and in Noss Mayo, is a small *Chapel of Ease*, erected in 1839. The benefice is a perpetual curacy, consolidated with the vicarage of Yealmpton. Here is 4A. 3R. 37P. of glebe, but no parsonage. The tithes have been commuted, the vicarial for £116, and the rectorial for £140 per annum. The trustees of the late Rev. J. Kenrick are lessees of the latter. The poor have a house and garden, purchased with £20, left by *Sir Wm. Hele*, in 1625, and other benefaction money.

In Noss Mayo, or as specified.

1850

Boden Mrs Sar.
Carter John, blacksmith
Elliott Sarah, beer seller
Kingcombe Hy. ferryman & cider dlr. *Passage House*
Kingcombe Geo. vict. Globe Inn
Leonard John, tailor
Merrill Wm. vict., Swan Inn
Pope John, carpenter, &c
Giles Sampson, R.N.

FARMERS.

Antony Jane, *Rowden*
Brooking Wm., *Revelstoke*
Crocker Henry, *Coombe*
Huxham George, *Netton*
Tuckett Jas. *Higher Coombe*
Wilcock John & Ann, *Worswell*

BAKERS.
Popham Humpy.
Kingcombe Jsh.
Sims Wm.

SHOPKEEPERS.
Perrett Phpi.
Walke Andrew
Williams John

BOOT & SHOE MKS.
Bunker Richard
Reeves Fredk.

1897

REVELSTOKE is a parish, on the south coast in Bigbury bay, 4 miles south from Yealmpton station on a branch and 10 south-west from Ivybridge station on the South Devon section of the main line of the Great Western railway, 10 south-east from Plymouth and 10 south from Plympton, in the Southern division of the county, hundred of Plympton, petty sessional division of Ermington and Plympton, union of Plympton St. Mary, county court district of East Stonehouse, rural deanery of Plympton, archdeaconry of Totnes and diocese of Exeter. The church of St. Peter, built in 1882, by Lord Revelstoke, at a cost of £29,000, from designs by Mr. J. P. St. Aubyn, architect, is an edifice of stone in the Perpendicular style, and consists of chancel, nave, aisles, south porch and an embattled western tower containing a clock with chimes and 8 bells: the seats, executed by Hems, of Exeter, are of solid oak handsomely carved, each bearing a different device: the font and the piers of the arcades are of granite: the stained west window was presented by the parishioners and the side windows of the chancel by the Rev. H. F. Roe M.A. rector 1871-90, and there are several in the south aisle to the Baring family, including one added in 1893, in memory of the late Louisa Emily Charlotte (Bulteel), wife of Lord Revelstoke, who died in 1892: the reredos, of Devonshire marble, is surmounted by a triptych representing "The Nativity" and "The Annunciation": the vestry is under the north transept: there are 250 sittings. The ancient and ivy-clad church of St. Peter, situated near Stoke Point close to the sea, is now in ruins, but since 1873 a portion has been repaired and fitted up, at a cost of £800, and is now used for burial services. The register dates from the year 1654. The living is a rectory, net yearly value £160, with 4 acres of glebe and residence, in the gift of the Bishop of Exeter, and held since 1890 by the Rev. William Eardley Roome M.A. of Corpus Christi College, Cambridge. Here is a Wesleyan chapel, and there is a reading room and library containing about 600 volumes, mostly presented by Lord Revelstoke. The population is chiefly at Noss Mayo, on the side of a creek adjacent to the mouth of the river Yealm and opposite to Newton Ferrers. Crabs, lobsters, pilchards and herrings are caught here in great abundance. This place since 1885 has given the title of baron to the Baring family. Lord Revelstoke is lord of the manor and principal landowner. The soil is very light; subsoil, mixed. The chief crops are wheat, barley and roots. The area is 1,541 acres of land, 40 of tidal water and 127 of foreshore; rateable value, £1,883; the population in 1891 was 470.

Parish Clerk, Nicholas Lobbs.

Letters received through Newton Ferrers from Plymouth at 8.30 a.m. & 3.50 p.m
Wall Letter Box at Noss Mayo, cleared at 5 p.m. week days only. The nearest money order & telegraph office is at Newton Ferrers, about 3 miles distant
Police Station, George B. Gatting, constable in charge
National School (mixed), built in 1839, for 200 children; average attendance, 120; Harold B. Plant, master
Carriers to Plymouth.—Henry Kingcombe & William Hockaday, tues. thurs. & sat. returning same days

Plant Harold B
Read Mrs
Roome Rev. Wm. Eardley M.A. Rectry

COMMERCIAL.

Elliott John, master mariner
Finch Frank, baker & grocer
Foster George, grocer & draper
Gill —, farmer, Netton
Hannaford Robert, farmer, Bowden
Hockaday Wm. shopkeeper & carrier
Kingcombe Henry, jun. carrier
Lewis George, Globe inn
Lobb Nicholas, farmer, High Coombe
Ralph Abraham, farmer, Worswell
Reading Room & Library (William Payne, librarian)
Rowe Aaron, baker
Sherrill & Co, blacksmiths
Sherrill William, Swan P.H
West William, foreman of works

The Globe Inn

Low tide, washing drying and smoke curling upwards from the inn and one or two houses adds to this early view when Harry Bidgood was the innkeeper. George Kingcombe and John Roe were at the inn prior to this photograph of about 1920.

Lot 26. (Coloured Pink on plan No. 2.)

"The Globe Inn"

Is entirely free, and has a full seven days' license.

It is built of Stone, Tiles, Cemented and with Slated Roof (being No. 13 on plan containing :—

On the Ground Floor—Tap Room with Bar and Small Room adjoining, and Kitchen

On the First Floor—Sitting Room communicating with Bed Room.

On the Second Floor—Three Bed Rooms.

The Garden of the "Globe" adjoins the Creek, and has a Large Stone and Tile Outhouse. Let to Mr. Bidgood on a yearly tenancy at a rental of £12 per annum Over the Tap Room is a Kitchen, Two Bed Rooms and a Wash-house (being No. 1 on plan). This with a portion of the Garden is let to Mrs. Edmonds on a yearly tenancy with other Lands at an apportioned rental of £3 10s. per annum.

The Garden adjoining the Globe Inn, and being No. 12a on plan, is at present let with No. 12 (Lot 24) to Mr. Axworthy and the apportioned rent will be 6s. per annum.

Included in this Lot is a Stone and Slated Store Room with Three Living Rooms over (being No. 21 on plan).

The Store Room is let with the Globe Inn, and the Three Living Rooms are let to Mr. Pearson on a yearly tenancy at a rental of £1 10s. per annum.

Also a Stone and Slated Cottage (being No. 20 on plan) containg Three Bed Rooms Living Room, Kitchen and Wash-house, Store Shed. Let to Mrs. J. Hartnell on a yearly tenancy at a rental of £4 15s. per annum.

The whole producing a total rental of

per £22 1s. annum.

Outgoings: Tenant of "The Globe" pays rates.

Lot 26
1915 Sale Details

The list of the accommodation and other details of the *Globe Inn* makes interesting reading especially in the light of many changes and charges over recent decades.

The Globe Inn

The once familiar circle on the side of the inn will be recalled by many people. Stores were kept in the building below it while the small building on the hillside was where Frederick Clarke, the butcher, slaughtered animals for his shop at Noss.

Point House

No traffic problems for the young child and dog outside this dwelling house where Mr. and Mrs. Jack Sims lived with their family. It was also a lodging house and occasionally people coming out to work would stay with the Sims. Next door is the well known bakery of Vincent Hodge. Ivy appears to have been allowed to grow over houses more so then than nowadays.

Looking down from Coombe Farm Road

At this period almost all the houses were owned by the Revelstoke estate but in 1915 a large sale enabled many of the local people to buy the property they were occupying. Mr. and Mrs. Reeve lived in the nearby house and further along was the carpenter, Mr. Bill Tope. The chimney stack and roof of the reading room can be easily recognised, then under the care of William Payne, while beyond stands the *Globe Inn* with Henry Bidgood in charge followed later by Charles Newton.

Newton Ferrers in the 1920s

Low water along the estuary throws into relief many of the old boats and crabbers on the shore which once used these waters. A gentle row up towards Newton sometime in this decade shows fields and thatched houses at the end of Riverside Road West. Holy Cross Church breaking the skyline was then the most prominent building of the village standing almost alone above its many houses.

The Point in View

The *Kitley Belle* is carefully turning by the Point sometime in the 1920s. *Harbour View* house was then occupied by Mr. Revel, the *Voss* is covered by high water, the old post office at Noss can be seen with its thatched roof close to the *Swan Inn*. Are one or two of the boats crabbers?

School children at Noss

Was this a break from school at Noss sometime before the First World War? Three of the boys are carrying pals on their backs and four girls are typically clothed in long white dresses. There is a crabber boat on the left; Mr. E. Dyer then lived in the house with the washing in its garden and Miss Lancaster, of the school, lived next to the gabled house. Mr. G. Andrews lived in the slated building.

Boats on the Waterfront

A few of the open boats are moored below Newton and what looks like a crabber is towards the right. The open field above the various dwellings has long gone but the village must have remained like this view for many years before changes came.

Many Boats on the Creek

There has been or will be plenty of activity on these waters if the number of boats are anything to go by. The *Globe Inn* can be recognised and Mr. Hodge's bakery remembered for not only its bread and cakes but for cooking the Sunday dinner when neighbours brought their meal and had it cooked in his oven. Mr. Sims then lived in the house on the right.

Large and Small Craft

A visitor's yacht overshadows the smaller locally-owned crabber. Edgar Foster recalls that his father bought a similar one, *Thistle*, from Salcombe for £14. Another, *May Queen*, was built at Bridgend. There were then twenty-seven crabbers working out from this estuary. The season always started on Valentine's Day, 14th February, and went through to September or October.

Getting the Boat Ready

Almost high water at Noss and an opportunity to get out of the narrow estuary for a day's crabbing probably on the East and West Rutts a favourite place for shell fish. The crabber is on the left and was usually fitted with a sprit sail and foresail. Two men would go out laying pots and then lifting them the following day. There was no fishing at all on Sundays!

Summer Houseboats

These were a feature of the estuary before the last war. People would modify a vessel so that they could sleep in it for weekends or have a holiday on it during the summer. The *Iris* houseboat is seen here then owned by Mr. Tope of Plymouth. This view is from the field at Ferry Cottage.

Low Tide at Noss

This very early view shows quite prominently the outbuildings which many houses had next to the tidal waters. These were used as toilets and stores and some had pigs in them which were killed for winter meat. This was quite a common practise many years ago. Both church towers of the locality can be seen with St. Peters framed by the tree felled many seasons ago.

Noss Creek Frontage

The allotments and fields date this view to the 1930s in which a small holiday building stands alone on the hillside. This was built by three ex-soldiers who vowed that they would meet together for holidays should they ever get out of the trenches during the First World War. Mr. James Harrison, headmaster, then lived next to gabled house; the building in front of the *Swan Inn* was burnt down and Edgar Foster can remember a chain of buckets being formed to quell the flames.

At work in the Creek

William Leonard, by the net-drying frame, Henry Foster, Jim Penwell and young Clarence Hodge have been identified by Edgar Foster. Mr. Penwell ran the carrier's van in his younger days. The boats are 14 feet in length and were used for ferrying passengers and generally getting around the estuary. Note the two crab pots on the foreshore just below the *Swan Inn*.

Bridgend Boat Yard
There has always been some kind of maritime activity here and this is being continued today. This early view shows the old malthouse, the quayside from where goods were brought in and taken out by a variety of vessels. There was also a blacksmith shop here and the swans seen here nested close to it. The malt was taken from here to Plymouth by boat for brewing.

Noss Mayo Primary School 1952
Children who performed for the school Christmas pantomime for that year were Christine Hall, Janet Gosling, Sian Thomas, Betty Pearse, Pam Bennett, Joyce Gosling, Michael Rowse, Paul Pearson, Andrew Trout, Trevor Finch, Ann Foster, Pamela Goodchild, Rita Martin, Caroline Messanger, Kinny Bradley, Diane Hall, Shirley Hosking, Brian Taylor, Rosemary Codd, Sylvia Delafield, Susan Roberts, Peggy Treneman and others.

Looking down Noss Creek
The cottages in the foreground were then occupied by Mr. and Mrs. W. Foster, Mr. and Mrs. T. Crook and Mr. H. Sims. *Harbour View*, opposite was the home of Mr. Revel and *Point Cottage* Mr. J. Sims. Newton is relatively undeveloped with fields at the level of Yealm Court Road and Wright's Lane.

No 1 Noss Mayo

Mr. and Mrs. Robert Mashford lived in the then ivy-clad house shown here with Ferry Cottage partly hidden in the background. This must be in the very early years of this century. Henry and Ann Kingcombe were recorded as occupying Ferry Cottage while Mr. Mashford was busily engaged in carrying corn, coal, etc. on his barges *The Brother* and *The Providence*. He was also skipper of *The Hornet* at one time. The coal came in from Plymouth and was sold by him locally.

Dressed for the Regatta

The importance of the annual summer regatta can be measured by the manner and style in which these people dress themselves. The view is at Wide Slip and it is sometime in the 1920s. There is a visiting steamer in the background and vessels are decked with flags.

9 mile Marathon

Charlie Axworthy is the winner on this occasion in the early 1920s of the nine mile Membland Drive marathon. Villagers turn out in large numbers to cheer him on while in the background the horse and trap was in readiness to pick up any runners who could not make the full distance. The corner house was once the butcher's shop at Noss.

Dancing along the Road

As part of the local celebrations for the coronation of King George VI in 1936, children and adults danced part way along the road to Passage Woods. These two pictures show some of the activities led by the persons playing the accordions in the lower one. A large flag drapes from a building in the top view.

Maypole Dancing at Playing Place

This spot in front of the school is known as *Playing Place* and the children are certainly doing this around the maypole on the occasion of the 1936 coronation.

Modbury Hounds

Noss is the meeting point for these hounds on this occasion and here they are assembling for a day's hunt at the head of the creek. The large van presumably brought out the hounds who are bounding about at the water's edge.

Outside the Tilley Institute

Mr. and Mrs. George Reeve are watching the celebrations of 1945 and a young boy holds the hand of maybe his father suitably attired for this occasion. Unfortunately the man has yet to be recognised.

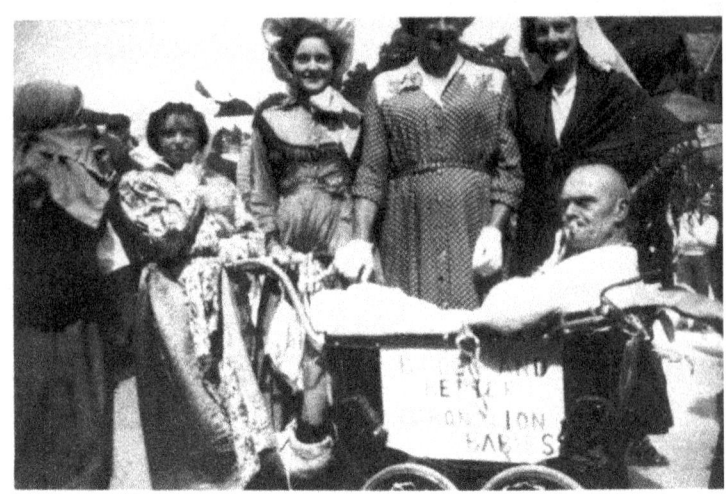

Coronation Celebrations in 1953

As part of the nation's celebrations at the crowning of Queen Elizabeth II in June, 1953, all kinds of local events were staged. Here George Bradley poses as a baby in the pram and behind him is Eileen and Margaret Crocker. Below an impersonation of a vicar is successfuly carried off by Ralph Hockaday with clasped hands.

1945 Peace Celebrations at Noss

The V.E. and V.J. celebrations were an occasion for people to get together and express their great joy and relief at the ending of the Second World War. Here many children and adults form a procession through part of the village.

Harvest Time at Rowden Farm

Its six farm workers, one being Mr. Reeve, stop for the camera and maybe food brought out by the two ladies in the very early years of the century. Farmer Stanley Paige leads part of the V.E. procession in 1945 riding, presumably, on one of his horses in the photograph shown on the left with local girls dancing behind him.

Donald Doddridge

He worked for Mr. Charlie Proctor at Newton Farm and is seen here delivering a cart load of horse manure to the large garden of Mrs. Wrights in Yealm Road, Newton. It is sometime in the late 1920s and her garden was behind the high brick wall. Mr. Cecil Lake recalls that this horse was a temperamental one which, if allowed, would always go round the Green at Newton instead of going straight on down from the farm. There were three farms at Newton. Newton, Court and Parsonage.

Membland Estate Sale

The extensive property of this estate included the Malthouse and Cottage at Bridgend. The sale notice is shown here which took place in 1915 at the Royal Hotel, Plymouth.

Lot 73. (Coloured Blue on Plan No. 3).

The Malthouse and Cottage

situated in the Parishes of Holbeton and Revelstoke.

The Malthouse is Stone and Slated and contains very Large Drying Floors with Furnace, the Cottage adjoins and contains Bed Room, Kitchen, and Storehouse.

There is also a Stone Slated Stable comprising Two Stalls, Coachhouse, Outhouse and a Fair Garden.

£37/0 Let to Messrs. William K. Pitts, Ltd., on a yearly tenancy at a rental of per **£30** annum.

The Garden Ground is at present let to Mrs. Lapthorn on a yearly tenancy, and the apportioned rental will be per 2s. 6d. annum.

Outgoings:

Tithe Commutation Rent Charge, Vicarial 8½d. Value 1915 6½d.

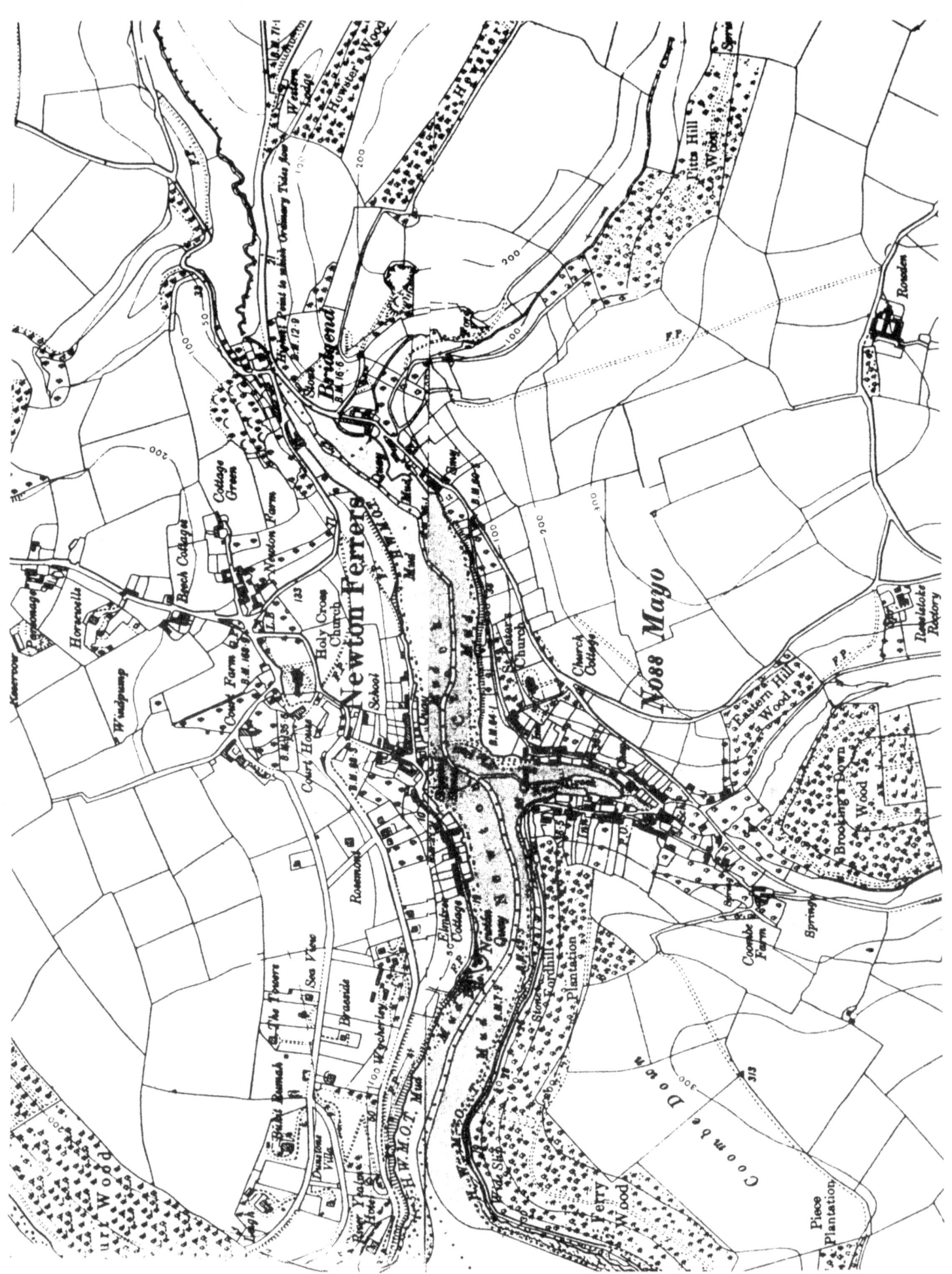

Arthur L. Clamp – the man behind the books

Arthur Leslie Clamp was a man of boundless energy with a passion for helping others, particularly through his love of history. A printer by trade, he started his career in a printing company before moving his family from Exeter to Plymouth to teach at the Plymouth College of Art and Design, where he eventually became the Head of the Printing Department.

Arthur with his five children.

A Devoted Family Man

Despite his love of teaching, Arthur prioritised his family, always making it home by 5:30pm for tea. He and his wife, Rosemary, raised five children: Susan, Angela, Elizabeth, David, and Steven. Arthur would often combine his love of family and history by taking his children on Sunday walks, encouraging them to appreciate historical monuments by taking photos or making crayon rubbings of gravestones for his books. The family home at 203 Elburton Road was a hub of activity, with a large garden, featuring a two-storey fort and a makeshift swimming pool.

A Lifelong Learner and Adventurer

Arthur's thirst for knowledge extended beyond history to a deep curiosity about the world. He was passionate about exploring different cultures, traditions, and cuisines, often taking advantage of his long summer holidays as a teacher to travel to places like India, Russia, South America, the middle east and the USA, sometimes bringing one of his children along. This adventurous spirit even influenced his home life, as seen by the short-lived family tradition of steam-cooking vegetables after a trip to Iceland.

History is a prominent feature of family days out

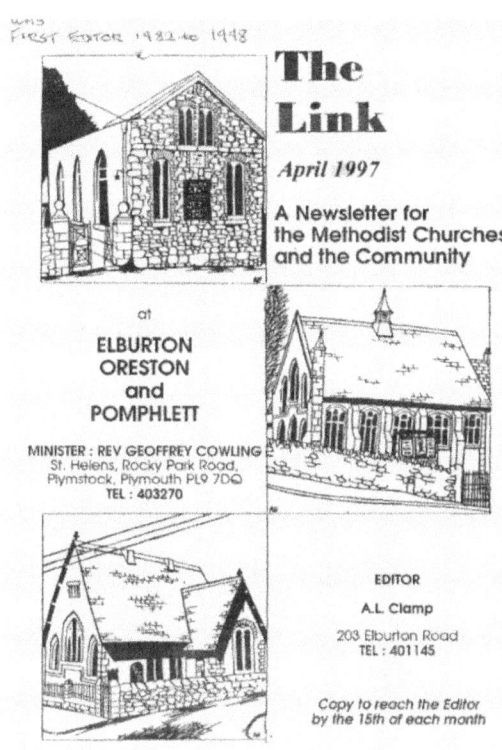

Community and Philanthropic Spirit

His commitment to serving others was evident in his long-standing involvement with the Elburton Methodist Church. He was the Sunday School Superintendent for over 15 years and served as the editor of the wider church's monthly newsletter, "The Link," for a similar duration. After Rosemary's very sad passing, Arthur later remarried and, following a chance encounter with a professor from India, established a connection with a missionary school in Chennai. Together with his new wife, Christine, he co-founded a "Sponsor a Child's Education" program that continues to this day.

Pictured left – The cover of 'The Link' complete with hand drawn sketches of each church by Angela
Below right – Arthur Clamp promoting his latest book
Below left – Arthur at home with his first wife, Rosemary
Below centre – Arthur on holiday with his second wife, Christine

A Legacy of Learning and Positivity

Arthur's greatest passion was history, which he brought to life through tireless research, documentation, and the many books he authored. He was driven by a need to "never be stuck in a rut," constantly seeking new experiences, meeting new people, and expanding his knowledge. With a positive attitude and a great sense of humour, he was always ready to help others, leaving a lasting impact on his family and community. His children, Susan, Angela, Elizabeth, David, and Steven, remember him with love and gratitude.

David Clamp, 2025

A Legacy of Local History

Below is the story of how Arthur L Clamp began writing books, in his own words, drafted shortly before he passed away in 2001. I have only made minor alterations to this text, correcting grammatical errors that he did not survive to correct himself. When I first discovered this text, I was shocked to see my name mentioned. It seems that, unbeknownst to me, I shared my first PC with him. I suspect he used it during the day when I was at school, although I do have one memory of sitting with him and showing him how it worked. It has been a pleasure to pick up where he left off and see his books republished and redistributed, and to know that I was part of the story, even back then. It was also fascinating to discover that his pricing structure matches the way I have tried to price the books, with a third going to local sellers and the rest covering printing costs with a little left over for my expenses.

I am his eldest grandson, and it is a privilege to curate his legacy, which we are calling 'The Clamp Collection'. The very last line of the text originally reads "The following pages list all the titles." Sadly, that page is missing and we have no record of all the books he published and knowing that some of those were researched by other authors makes the process of finding them even harder. I look forward to one day completing the collection and seeing them all available again. And maybe, one day, I'll even start writing my own to add to the series. For now, here is his story in his own words.

Steven Gibson, 2025

Writing and Publishing Booklets on Local Topics and Areas

I started this interest in either 1968 or 1969 when living in Woodford. I had by these dates established the Department of Printing and I think I must have been looking for something different to do. The first titles were of A5 size proofed from type set at Clarke, Doble and Brendon, Ltd., Plymouth printers, and then made up into pages and printed at Sawtell and Neilson, Ltd., Totnes.

Then began a slow process of getting them out to shops, etc. which proved to be more time consuming and difficult than actually researching, writing and getting the books into print. However, I persisted and opened a business account with Barclays Bank on the Broadway. I was advised to give it a title so I called it "Westway Publications". There came along another problem, one of storage of paper and finished books which was solved when the family moved to Elburton in 1970.

I changed the printer to Penwell, Ltd., Callington, Cornwall, as he was then just setting up himself and his prices seemed very reasonable. I did not get any of the printers to make up the complete books. I hand folded the flat printed sheets, stitched the books on a small manual table stitcher and trimmed them in a small hand turned guillotine which I bought from someone in Penzance for £40. It was brought up in a van.

The trouble and time going to and fro to Callington was too much so I transferred the printing to PDS Printers, Prince Rock, Plymouth, and I have been with them ever since. Now they are at Plympton which is easy to reach and they fold the flat sheets which was turning out to be a long chore which only saved a small part of the printing costs.

All my first titles were written by myself. I took the photographs and developed them in the loft of the house, the type was set by now on a computer situated in the house at Elburton from which I had collected photographic lengths of text to cut up and law down as pages.

At some point I decided that I would do my own film processing of lith film so I bought a large second hand process camera from Kingsbridge and learnt through trial and error to make line negatives of the text and halftone negatives of the illustrations which proved more difficult than I anticipated. The main problem was trying to keep the developer in the large dish at the correct temperature as any change would affect the developing time. I replaced this old camera with a brand new one bought from Croydon, Surrey, costing £900. This has turned out to be a great asset cutting out an expensive part of the printer's costs and one crucial aspect of the work which I could control.

By the middle 1970s there were many outlets I had contacted in Plymouth, up to Dartmoor, Exeter, around to Torbay, Totnes, Dartmouth and the South Hams. The market for local books was much greater than I had first thought and through getting to know many local people undertaking research themselves had the chance to help and make up books for other people who had in most instances, got together a collection of photographs with some text in a rather muddled way. Through my experience in print I was able to shape up their work and get it into print and in every case I had to pay the printer and let the person have the royalties. In the majority of titles produced in this manner this was another way of producing titles and it did give some profit to my work. However, I must say that in a few cases I lost out by either the other person getting the numbers wrong, not returning any monies from stock I delivered or they thought that more of their books should have been sold.

The print run was usually 1,000 copies and from time to time I have had reprints of 250 copies. It took about ten years to clear the first print run so I always had large stocks in the garage, workshop, etc. The numbers sold during the early years was about 7,000 copies a year increasing to around 9,000 copies and for the whole of the enterprise about 500,000 have been sold. The booklets have become part of the local scene and many people collect them, shops regularly order copies and I go around certain areas month by month restocking or replacing titles as necessary.

During the past year or so I have started setting the text on a Packard Bell PC, something which I should have done some years back. I share it with Steven Gibson, my grandson. There appears to be no end to the market for local books, but I could not earn a regular income because of the long time it takes to sell stock.

However, now exceeding 100 titles made up mainly of A4 twenty-four page booklets, some folded guides, with selling prices set with a third going to the shop which is the trade custom, the original idea has been quite successful and could go on for ever.

Apart from monetary benefits, however spasmodically these might be, I have learnt a lot myself, met many interesting people and have become part of the local scene with requests to give talks and to advise people about getting into print.

Arthur L Clamp, 2001

Death of local historical author

'He was an incredible character who was just loved by everybody who knew him'

A WELL-loved Elburton author has died at the age of 68.

Arthur Clamp (pictured right), who was one of the West Country's most successful writers, died at St Luke's Hospice, Turnchapel, after losing his battle against cancer.

Tributes have been flooding in for a man who was known in the community as a prominent writer and outgoing person.

He produced more than 140 titles during his life, dealing with both fiction, fact and history, often discussing West Country topics that were close to his heart.

One of his most acclaimed books was The Plymouth Blitz, and he also credit it for The Rise and Fall of the Bearings of Membland Hall, set in Noss Mayo.

He achieved sales of between 7,000 and 9,000 books every year and it is estimated that he has sold over half a million books, covering the areas of Plymouth, Dartmoor, Exeter, Torbay and the South Hams.

Mr Clamp was born in Mitcham, Surrey, in 1932, and was the eldest of four children.

He moved to Devon in 1941 to avoid the London air-raids.

Mr Clamp trained as a printer in Exeter and also gained a teachers' certificate in 1959 from Garnet College in London.

Plymouth College of Art, however, was to prove to be Mr Clamp's working home for the following 32 years until 1991, when he retired as head of the printing department.

He had a great interest in travel and had visited the USA, Tanzania, China, Russia, Peru, as well as travelling across Europe, where he presented talks and slide shows on his experiences as a writer.

Mr Clamp was a member of Elburton Methodist Church for many years, superintendent of the Sunday school and editor of the church newsletter, as well as being involved in much charity work.

He was president of the Plymouth and District Field Club and an active member of the Elburton Residents' Association.

He enjoyed leading walks on Dartmoor and historical tours throughout the West Country.

Mr Clamp married his first wife, Rosemary, in 1956 and they had five children – Susan, Angela, Elizabeth, David and Steven – and she died in 1987. He also had 11 grandchildren.

He leaves a wife Christine, after remarrying in 1991, and her two children and three grandchildren.

'He was an incredible character who was just loved by everybody who knew him,' said his wife.

'He will be missed by his family, his friends, the people he worked with and just everybody who knew him through his books.'

More than 300 mourners attended his funeral at Elburton Methodist Church on Monday.

The attendance was a celebration of his life – he would have found that really special. It shows his vibrancy and love of people,' said Mrs Clamp.

Steven Clamp added that his father was 'a well respected and loved man, missed by a great many people throughout the South West and far beyond'.

This newspaper article, published by the Evening Herald on 17th August 2001, forms a good record of his life. Just as he encourages us to learn more about local history, we encourage you to learn a little about him. For that reason, we have included these pages at the back of all the most recently republished books, in honour of his memory and recognition of his contribution to the community.

www.ingramcontent.com/pod-product-compliance
Lightning Source LLC
Chambersburg PA
CBHW061404070526
44584CB00031B/4158